The Female Soldier; Or, The Surprising Life *And* Adventures Of *Hannah Snell*

By

Anonymous

Roza Shanina, a Soviet sniper during World War II

North Korean Female Navy recruits

The Social Revolution--Felicien Rops

Born in the CITY of *Worcester*,

Who took upon herself the Name of *James Gray*; and, being deserted by her Husband, put on Mens Apparel, and travelled to *Coventry* in quest of him, where she enlisted in Col. *Guise*'s Regiment of Foot, and marched with that Regiment to *Carlisle*, in the Time of the

Rebellion in *Scotland*; shewing what happened to her in that City, and her Desertion from that Regiment.

ALSO

A Full and True ACCOUNT of her enlisting afterwards into *Fraser*'s Regiment of Marines, then at *Portsmouth*; and her being draughted out of that Regiment, and sent on board the *Swallow* Sloop of War, one of Admiral *Boscawen*'s Squadron, then bound for the *East-Indies*. With the many Vicissitudes of Fortune she met with during that Expedition, particularly at the Siege of *Pondicherry*, where she received Twelve Wounds. Likewise, the surprising Accident by which she came to hear of the Death of her faithless Husband, who she went in quest of.

TOGETHER

With an ACCOUNT of what happened to her in the Voyage to *England*, in the *Eltham* Man of War. The whole containing the most surprizing Incidents that have happened in any preceding Age; wherein is laid open all her Adventures, in Mens Cloaths, for near five Years, without her Sex being ever discovered.

LONDON:
Printed for, and Sold by R. WALKER, the Corner of *Elliot's-Court*, in the *Little Old-Bailey*. 1750. Price One Shilling.

TO THE
PUBLICK.

N*otwithstanding the surprizing Adventures of this our* British *Heroine, of whom the following Pages fully and impartially treat; yet the Oddity of her Conduct for preserving her Virtue was such, that it demands not only Respect, but Admiration; and as there is nothing to be found in the following Sheets, but what is Matter of Fact, it merits the Countenance and Approbation of every Inhabitant of this great Isle, especially the Fair Sex, for whom this Treatise is chiefly intended; and the Truth of which being confirmed by our Heroines Affidavit, made before the Right Hon. the Lord Mayor, the said Affidavit is hereunto annexed, in order to prevent the Publick from being imposed upon by fictitious Accounts.*

Hannah Snell, *born in the City of* Worcester, *in the Year of our Lord 1723, and who took upon her the Name of* James Gray, *maketh Oath, and saith, That she this Deponent served his present Majesty King* George, *as a Soldier and Sailor, from the 27th of* November, *One Thousand Seven Hundred and Forty five, to the 9th of this Instant* June, *and entered herself as a Marine in Capt.* Graham*'s Company in Col.* Fraser*'s Regiment, and went on board the* Swallow, *his Majesty's Sloop of War, to the* East-Indies, *belonging to Admiral* Boscawen*'s Squadron, where this Deponent was present at the Siege of* Pondicherry, *and all the other Sieges during that Expedition, in which she received Twelve Wounds, some of which were dangerous, and was put into the Hospital for Cure of the same, and returned into* England *in the* Eltham *Man of War, Capt.* Lloyd *Commander, without the least Discovery of her Sex.*

And this Deponent further maketh Oath, and saith, That she has delivered to Robert Walker, *Printer, in the* Little Old-Bailey, London, *a full and true Account of the many surprizing Incidents, and wonderful Hardships she underwent during the Time she was in his Majesty's Service as aforesaid, to be by him printed and published.*

And this Deponent lastly saith, That she has not given the least Hint of her surprising Adventures to any other Person, nor will she, this Deponent, give any the Least Account thereof, to any Person whatsoever, to be printed or published, save and except the above-mentioned Robert Walker.

Sworn before me this 27th Day of *June*, 1750, at *Goldsmith's Hall, London*,

J. BLACHFORD, Mayor.

Witness

Susannah Gray,
Sister of the said Hannah Snell.
T. Edwards.

Her
Hannah x Snell,
Mark.

THE LIFE AND ADVENTURES OF
Hannah Snell, &c.

n this dastardly Age of the World, when Effeminacy and Debauchery have taken Place of the Love of Glory, and that noble Ardor after warlike Exploits, which flowed in the Bosoms of our Ancestors, genuine Heroism, or rather an extraordinary Degree of Courage, are Prodigies among Men. What Age, for Instance, produces a *Charles* of *Sweden*, a *Marlborough*, or a Prince *Eugene*? These are *Rara Aves in Terris*, and when they appear, they seem to be particularly designed by Heaven, for protecting the Rights of injured Nations, against foreign Oppression, securing the Privileges of Innocence from the dire Assault of Prey and Rapine; and, in a Word, vindicating the common Prerogatives of human Nature, from the fatal Effects of brutal Rage, the love of Conquest, and an insatiable Lust after Power. The amazing Benefit arising to Mankind from such illustrious and exalted Characters, is, perhaps, the principal Reason why they attract the Eyes, and command the Attention of all who hear of them, even in Quarters of the World far remote from their Influence and Sphere of Action: Why they are the Subjects of the Poets Song, the Founders of the Historian Narration, and the Objects of the Painters Pencil; all which have a Tendency to transmit their Names with immortal Glory to latest Ages, and eternize their Memories, when their Bodies are mouldred into Dust, and mingled with their Parent Earth. Perhaps their Rarity may also contribute, in a great Measure, to that Esteem and Veneration, which the World thinks fit to pay them: But sure if Heroism, Fortitude, and a Soul equal to all the glorious Acts of War and Conquest, are Things so rare, and so much admired among Men; how much rarer, and consequently how much more are they to be admired among Women? In short, we may on this Occasion, without any Hyperbole, use the Words of *Solomon*, and say, *One Man among a thousand have I found, but among Women not so*. However, tho' Courage and warlike Expeditions, are not the Provinces by the World allotted to Women since the Days of the *Amazons*, yet the female Sex is far from being destitute of Heroinism. *Cleopatra* headed a noble Army against *Mark Anthony*, the greatest Warrior of his Time. *Semiramis* was not inferior to her in Courage.
The *Arcadian* Shepherdesses are as memorable for their Contempt of Danger as their darling and beloved Swains. But among all our Heroines, none comes more immediately under our Cognizance, nor, perhaps, more merits our Attention than

the remarkable *Hannah Snell*, whose History is highly interesting, both on Account of the Variety of amazing Incidents, and the untainted Veracity with which it is attended. Some People guided rather by the Suggestions of Caprice, than the Dictates of Reason and a sound Understanding, have foolishly imagin'd, that Persons of low and undistinguished Births, hardly ever rais'd themselves to the Summit of Glory and Renown; but they will find themselves widely mistaken, when they reflect on a *Kauli-Kan*, a *Cromwell*, and many others I could mention. But if this Observation had the smallest Foundation either in Nature or the Course of human Experience, from the most remote, to the present Age, yet its Force does by no Means extend to *Hannah Snell*, the Heroine of the subsequent Narrative: For though her immediate Progenitors were but low in the World, when compared with Dukes, Earls and Generals, yet she had the Seeds of Heroism, Courage and Patriotism transferr'd to her from her Ancestors, as will appear from the following Account of her Genealogy.

HANNAH SNELL, was born in *Fryer-Street*, in the Parish of *St. Hellen*'s, in the City of *Worcester*, on the 23d Day of *April*, 1723. Her Parents, tho' not immensely Rich by the hereditary Gifts of Fortune, yet secured a Competency, which not only placed them above Contempt, but also enabled them to bring up, and educate a numerous Family, none of whom have miscarried for want either of sufficient Learning from Masters, or salutary Advices and virtuous Examples from their Parents. And though Mrs. *Hannah Snell* did not while she was at School learn to write, yet she made a tolerable Progress in the other Part of Education common to her Sex, and could read exceeding well.

THOUGH the Father of our Heroine was no more than a *Hosier* and *Dyer*, yet he was the Son of the illustrious Capt. Lieut. *Sam. Snell*, for so I may or rather must call him, since with Intrepidity he stood the Brunt of the Wars in the latter End of King *William*'s Reign, signalized himself at the taking of *Dunkirk* and served faithfully in the *English* Army during Queen *Anne*'s Wars.

THIS Captain Lieutenant *Snell*, the Grandfather of our Heroine, enter'd as a Volunteer in King *William*'s Reign, and in the Beginning of Queen *Anne*'s Wars, was at the taking of *Dunkirk* under the Duke of *Marlborough*, where the Captain Lieutenant was killed by a Shot fired through the Wicket by the Governor; upon which he fired, and killed the Governor. When the Duke was informed thereof, he called him, and asked him what Preferment he desired; his Answer was, that he chose to accept of that Commission, which was become vacant by the Death of the Captain Lieutenant, which he was immediately preferr'd to, and took upon him the Command as such. After the Surrender of *Dunkirk*, where he received several dangerous Wounds, he returned to *England*, where he had the proffer of a very handsome Pension in *Chelsea College*; but coveting fresh Glory, and new Trophies of Conquest, he intreated of his Grace, that he would permit him once more to go Abroad with him, that he might have an Opportunity of signalizing his Valour, against the avowed Enemies of his Country. This his Request his Grace complied with, and at the Battle of *Malplaquet* he received a mortal Wound, from whence he was carried to *Ghent*, where he died: This last, was the twenty-second bloody Battle in which he had been engaged, and which he generously launched out into upon the sublime Motives, Liberty and Property. This Gentleman's Character must appear the more sublime, when we observe how he advanced himself by Merit from a private *Cadit* to the Rank he held at his Death; and had it not been for his over-modest and generous Sentiments, he might have been preferr'd to a much higher Rank; but the*Englishman* prevail'd above Self-Interest.

The Son of this illustrious Man of whom we have here treated, and Father of our Heroine, was possessed of many excellent Gifts, particularly Courage, for which he was distinguished; yet never had an Opportunity of displaying his Bravery in the Field of Battle, his Genius leading him another Way, to wit, Trade, into which he entered very young, and prospered in the World, married to his liking, and in a few Years saw himself the Father of nine promising Children, three of which were Sons, and six Daughters, all of whom save one Daughter, were either Soldiers or Sailors, or intermarried with them. The eldest of the Sons,*Samuel Snell*, incapable of Restraint, and void of all Fear, listed himself a Soldier in Lord *Robert Manners*'s Company in the first Regiment of Foot-Guards, commanded by his Royal Highness the Duke of *Cumberland*; when he was draughted to go for *Flanders*, where he received his mortal Wound at the battle of*Fontenoy*; and being sent to the Hospital at *Doway*, he there expired.

T H O ' the Daughters were, by those who knew them, accounted aimable Women, both on Account of their Persons and their Virtue; yet I shall pass over the Characters of five of them in Silence, and only take Notice of that of *Hannah*, the youngest of them but one, who is the Heroine of this Subject. It is a common Thing to observe a Family dispersed, when the Heads of that Family are either laid in their Graves, or by accidental Calamities rendered incapable of supporting it longer. Accordingly, when the Father and Mother of *Hannah* died, *Hannah* came up to *London*, and arrived in Town on *Christmas-Day*, 1740, and resided for some Time, with her Sister in *Wapping*.

S O M E Time after she came to *London*, she contracted an Acquaintance with one *James Summs*, a Sailor, who was a *Dutchman*; this Acquaintance was gradually improved into a Familiarity, and this Familiarity soon created a mutual, tho' not a criminal Passion; for in a little Time, *Summs* made his Addresses to her as a Lover, and gained her Consent, and was married to her at the *Fleet*, on the sixth Day of *January*, 1743-4. But all his Promises of Friendship, proved Instances of the highest Perfidy, and he turn'd out the worst and most unnatural of Husbands. Since, tho' she had Charms enough to captivate the Heart, and secure the Affection of any reasonable Man, yet she was despised and contemned by her Husband, who not only kept criminal Company with other Women of the basest Characters, but also made away with her Things, in Order to support his Luxury, and the daily Expences of his Whores. During this unlucky Period of the Husband's Debauchery, she poor Woman proved with Child, and at the same Time felt all the Shocks of Poverty, without exposing her Necessities to her nearest Friends. But at last, her Pregnancy laid the Foundation for her passing through all the Scenes, thro' which she has wandered; for when she was seven Months gone with Child, her perfidious Husband finding himself deeply involv'd in Debt, made an Elopement from her. Notwithstanding these her Calamities, she patiently bore herself up under them, and in two Months after her Husband's Departure was delivered of a Daughter which lived no more than seven Months, and was decently interred at her own Expence at *St. George*'s Parish in *Middlesex*.

FROM the Time of her Husband's Elopement till the Time she put on Man's Cloaths, she continued with her Sister, who is married to one *James Gray*, a House Carpenter, in *Ship-street, Wapping*, and from whence she took her Departure unknown to any, and was never heard of until her Return; and with whom she now dwells.

As she was now free from all the Ties arising from Nature and Consanguinity; she thought herself privileged to roam in quest of the Man, who, without Reason, had injured her so much; for there are no Bounds to be set either to Love, Jealousy or Hatred, in the female Mind. That she might execute her Designs with the better Grace, and the more Success, she boldly commenced a Man, at least in her Dress, and no doubt she had a Right to do so, since she had the real Soul of a Man in her Breast. Dismay'd at no Accidents, and giving a full Scope to the genuine Bent of her Heart, she put on a Suit of her Brother-in-Law, Mr. *James Gray*'s, Cloaths, assumed his Name, and set out on the 23d of *November*, 1745, and travelled to *Coventry*, with a View of finding her Husband, where she enlisted on the 27th of the said Month of *November*, in General *Guise*'s Regiment, and in the Company belonging to Captain *Miller*.

WITH this Regiment she marched from *Coventry* to *Carlisle*, where she learned her military Exercise, which she now performs with as much Skill and Dexterity as any Serjeant or Corporal in his Majesty's Service. But here, as Fortune is often a Foe to the Distressed, she met with a discouraging Circumstance; for her Serjeant, whose Name was *Davis*, having a criminal Inclination for a young Woman in that Town, looked upon this our Female Heroine, (a common Soldier in the Company) as a proper Person for assisting him in this his vicious Intrigue, therefore disclosed to her this Bosom Secret, and desired her Endeavours in promoting this End; however, this open Discovery caused a sudden Emotion in her Mind, her virtuous Soul abhorred with a becoming Detestation the criminal Intention; yet to prevent the ill Consequences that she foresaw must ensue from a refusal of complying with his Request, she promised to use her Endeavours in his Behalf; but instead of acting the Pimp, she went and disclosed the whole Matter to the young Woman, and warned her against the impending Danger; which Act of Virtue and Generosity in a Soldier, gained her the Esteem and Confidence of this young Woman, who took great delight in her Company; and seldom a Day passed but they were together, having cultivated an Intimacy and Friendship with each other:

But *Davis* going one Day to make his Addresses to his Mistress, met with an unexpected Repulse, which unusual Treatment made him suspect our Female Soldier. Jealousy that Moment took Possession of his guilty Breast, and he imagined, that instead of befriending him in his Amours, she had become his Rival, and had gained her over to her Inclinations. These Reflections troubled him much; Revenge reigned triumphant in his Breast, and how to punish her was his chief Aim: He took hold of the earliest Opportunity, and accused her before the commanding Officer for Neglect of Duty, upon which she was sentenced to receive six hundred Lashes, five hundred of which she received, having her Hands tied to the Castle Gates for a Crime which Nature put it out of her Power to perpetrate, and had undergone the Punishment of the other Hundred, had it not been for the Intercession of some of the Officers. This severe and unjust Punishment, reduced her to a very low State, but notwithstanding this severe Whipping, the Villain *Davis* bore her an implacable Hatred, and strove all he could to depress her, by putting her upon the hardest and most difficult Duties; but she was most tenderly and affectionately regarded by her Female Friend, who neglected nothing that might assure her, she was neither unmindful nor ungrateful for the Friendship she had shewed her. Soon after this, a fresh and unforeseen Trouble presented itself; there happened to come a fresh Recruit to the Regiment, a young Man whose Name was *George Beck*, a Carpenter, born in *Worcester* City, that had come to *London* in Quest of Business, and happened to lodge with her Brother and Sister, and whom she left at her Brothers House when she went off in Men's Cloaths, the Sight of whom troubled her much, fearing she should be discovered by him; this, together with the Serjeant's ill Treatment, inspired her with a Resolution to desert; having carried this her Intention to Maturity, she communicated the same to her intimate Friend the young Woman, who, tho' loth to lose the Company of such a Friend and Companion, yielded to her Remonstrances, and provided her with Money to bear her Charge in her intended Flight.

HAVING gone so far with the Author of this Subject, I cannot refrain making a little Digression, and making a few Reflections upon the melancholy Prospect: What an Ocean of Troubles was this unfortunate Woman involved in? Behold her inwardly looking back on the past Vicissitudes of her Life, on an inhumane, ungrateful and faithless Husband, who had broke through all Engagements, sacred and civil, and had drove her into all the direful Troubles and Afflictions she was then involved in: Behold her tempted by a vicious Man, to be aiding and assisting in carrying on an immodest and abominable Intrigue; but (being inspired with virtuous and generous Sentiments) she proved the Instrument of extracting Good out of Evil, in discovering to the innocent Maid, where the Net was spread for her, that she might guard her self against the Adversary: Behold the Friendship that this virtuous Discovery produced, it chained them together in the strictest Bonds of Love and Affection, which never quitted its hold, till forced thereto by a hard Fate: Behold her suspected of supplanting the Serjeant of his Mistress, and the direful Effects his Jealousy occasioned, having her Arms extended, and fixed to the City Gates, and there receive the Number of five hundred severe Lashes, as the Effects of a partial and unjust Sentence: Behold her tender Flesh cut and mangled by these Scourgings, and the Pains and Agonies she suffered: Behold in this her Distress, the friendly Sympathy and eager Assistance of her female Friend, who administred Relief to her under this her Dilemma: Behold the Commotions she felt upon perciving one in the Regiment whom she knew, and by whom she was afraid of being discovered; the bad Treatment she met with from the Serjeant, and what a Storm must surround her upon her projecting the Means for an Escape, and the moving Seperation 'twixt her and her Friend: The Rehearsal of so many concurring Circumstances of Adversity, is sufficient to melt the most stoney Heart into a compassionate Tenderness for this our female Adventurer.

HAVING finished this Digression, I shall begin where I left off. Upon her Desertion, she set out on Foot for *Portsmouth*, and about a Mile out of *Carlisle*, exchanges her regimental Clothes for worse, with some People employed in cutting down Pease. But Courage and Love, like impetuous Torrents, rage the more they are opposed; for *Hannah* whose Breast was actuated with both these Principles, had no sooner arrived at *Portsmouth*, than she found her Expectations disapointed: However, whether Despair or the Hopes of again meeting that unfaithful Man, who had made her the Mother of a helpless Infant, actuated her Breast and gave her Passions a preternatural Spring. So it was, that she courageously inlisted herself in Captain *Graham*'s Company in Colonel*Fraser*'s Regiment, and soon after there was a Draught made, to go abroad in

Admiral *Boscawen*'s Fleet, and she chanced to be one of the Number draughted, and went immediately on board the *Swallow* Sloop, Captain *Rosier*, Commander; and when on board was observed to be handy in washing, as well as in dressing Victuals, for the Mess she first belonged to, and being thus remarkable, she was sollicited by *Richard Wyegate*, Lieutenant of Marines, to become one of their Mess, which she readily agreed to, as believing the Officers Mess, was better than the common Mens, and she acted in the Station of their Boy, and by her modest Deportment soon became a Favourite, drest their Victuals, washed and mended their Linnen. She was stationed (in Case of an Engagement) on the Quarter-Deck, and to fight at small Arms, and made one of the After-Guard; she was obliged to keep watch four Hours on and four off, Day and Night, being often obliged to go aloft, and altho' unexperienced with these Kind of Hardships, soon became expert in the Business.

ON their first setting sail, they enjoyed as fine Weather, and as fair Winds as could possibly be wished for, to convey a Ship safely and expeditiously from one Harbour to another. But no sooner were they arrived in the Bay of *Biscay* than the Scene was altered; their favourable Weather converted into a dismal Hurricane, and their smooth placed Ocean, changed into Billows, which threaten'd them with immediate Death, by this Moment raising them to the Clouds, and in the next plunging them, as it were, to the Centre of the Earth. The Danger may be easily estimated, from the Circumstance, for the *Swallow* was as strong and well built a Vessel, as any belonging to his Majesty's Navy of her Burden: yet such was the Stress of Weather, that she sprung her Main-mast, and lost not only the Gib-Boom, but also two Top-masts. After they had for several Days been beat about in this imminent Danger, they with great Difficulty arrived in the Port of *Lisbon*, which was great Joy to them, after having suffered so much in the Bay of *Biscay*, where every Moment they had been in danger of being swallowed up in the vast Abyss. In this Port, which to them was like a safe Asylum, or Sanctuary, to a Man pursued by a hungry and enraged Lyon, they continued three Weeks; because the Vessel was so damaged, that the Number of Hands employed in refitting her could not do it sooner.

HERE they found the *Vigilant* Man of War, which was likewise much damaged in the Storm in the Bay of *Biscay*, being one of the Fleet that sail'd from*Portsmouth* with them.

WHILE she was ashore at *Lisbon*, with her Master, she was quartered at one Mrs. *Poore*'s a Punch-House and Tavern; but says nothing material happened there, during the three Weeks.

As it often happens for the wise and noble Purposes of Heaven, that one Misfortune succeeds another, as close as the Waves on the Sea-shore; so the *Swallow* set sail in Company with the *Vigilant* Man of War, in Order to join the Admiral's Squadron; and the next Night after their Departure, another violent Storm happened, in which the *Swallow* not only lost sight of the *Vigilant*, but also sprung her Main-mast, lost most of her Rigging, and was so much damaged in her Hold, that all the Sailors and Marines were obliged to take their several Turns at the Pump, which is by far a harder Piece of Labour, than those who have never tried it are apt to imagine. Such a Series of Calamities succeeding each other so fast, and so unexpectedly, were, in all Appearance, sufficient to daunt the strongest Resolution, and cool the Courage of the bravest young Sailor that ever trod the Deck of a Ship. But some Minds are cast, if I may so speak, in so happy a Mould, that Danger and Difficulties instead of depressing, raise them above themselves, enlarge their Views, and animate them to stem the Tide of Adversity, which they rarely fail to surmount by Steadiness and Perseverance. To this favourite Class of Mortals our Heroine belonged, since on this Occasion she not only willingly took her Turn at the Pump of a sinking Vessel, but also performed the several Offices of a common Sailor, and in both Qualities behaved with such Judgment and Intrepidity, that, next under God, she was looked upon by the Ship's Company as a Kind of Deliverer, and an Instrument of their Preservation. The *Swallow* after this Disaster made the best of her Way to *Gibraltar*, were as soon as they arrived, she went on Shore, and attended Lieutenant *Richard Wigate*, Lieutenant of the Marines, who was very ill, and lodged at Mrs. *Davis*'s on the Hill.

THE Ship refitted here with the utmost Expedition, and sailed for the *Madiera* Islands, where she took in such Wines, and other Provisions, as was thought necessary for the intended Voyage. As Providence is always Kind to Distress, she here met with the *Sheerness* Privateer of *Bristol*, whose Commander generously supplied her with a sufficient Number of Hands, and from thence, they sailed to the Cape of *Good Hope*, and in their Voyage, were put upon Short, and some time after upon Half Allowance.

DURING their Passage, their Allowance was shortened, as I just beforementioned, and that which they had, was salt and bad, and besides there was so great a Scarcity of Water on board, that they were allowed only a Pint a Day for some Time; all which, must have been great Hardships to her.

WHEN they arrived at the Cape, they there met with the Admiral in the *Namur*, which was great Joy to them; and our Heroine being disappointed hitherto of meeting her faithless Husband, and now seeing the Fleet all in Company, was in hopes of acquiring some Glory as a Soldier, knowing the Reason of this Fleet's being fitted out was to annoy the Enemies of her Country, which soon happened according to her Wishes, as the Fleet soon sailed from this Port for *Morusus*, on which Place they began their first Attack; and though unexperienced in the Use of Arms, except in learning her Exercise, she behaved with an uncommon Bravery, and exerted herself in her Country's Cause.

THIS Attack did not hold long; our brave Admiral finding this impracticable, and unwilling to lose his Ships and Men, for whom he had great Regard, left that Place, and sailed for Fort St. *David*'s, where they arrived in a little Time, and the Marines being put on Shore joined the *English* Army, and encamped, and in about three Weeks marched and encamped before *Elacapong*, and laid Siege to it, with an Intent to storm the Place. This fresh Adventure inspired her with fresh Hopes of shewing her undaunted Courage, which she did to the Admiration of her Officers; but on the tenth Day of the Siege, a Shell from the *English* took the Magazine of the Enemy, and blew it up, which occasioned them to surrender at Discretion.

I CANNOT help reflecting a little upon the Hardships, Fatigues and Dangers she incountered from the Time she left *Lisbon* in *Europe*, till her Arrival before *Pondicherry* in *Asia*, so many Vicissitudes, as were sufficient to damp the Spirits of an *Alexander* or a *Cæsar*, Storms, Hurricanes and pinching Want, were her Concomitants, pumping an almost wrecked Vessel, was her most constant (tho' laborious) Employment; seventeen Weeks short Allowance from the *Maderas* to the *Cape* of *Good Hope*, was all she had to subsist upon; Attacks upon fortified Towns, some of which were impregnable, where Bomb-Shells and Cannons were incessantly displaying Death wherever they fell; at other Times, moving, marching, and encamping; I say such Reflections and gloomy Prospects, prove the Cause of many such Hardships and Difficulties even in the most robust of the Masculine Gender, how much more in one of the tender Sex, who are afraid of Shaddows, and shudders at the Pressage of a Dream.

I SHALL now proceed to their March to *Pondicherry*, which is but a few Leagues from the forementioned Place; they encamped within about three Miles from the Town, *Boscawen* being then both Admiral and General, and Major *Mount Pleasant* informed them with their Intention, which was to storm the Place, which Attack was began by the Ships firing at the Fort, some of which Time they lay Middle-deep in Water in their Trenches: This Attack continued eleven Weeks, part of which Time they had no Bread, most of their Food being Rice; and the many Bombs and Shells thrown among them, killed and wounded many of their Men. During this Space of Time, she behaved with the greatest Bravery and Intrepidity, such as was consistent with the Character of an *English* Soldier, and though so deep in Water, fired 37 Rounds of Shot, and received a Shot in the Groin, six Shots in one Leg, and five in the other.

THE Siege being now broke up, by reason of the heavy Rains, and violent Claps of Thunder, it being the Time of the Year when the *Monzoons* (for so they are called in that Country) happens, she was sent to an Hospital at *Cuddylorom*, under the Care of two able Physicians, *viz.* Mr. *Belchier* and Mr. *Hancock*; but she, not willing to be discovered, extracted the Ball out of her Groin herself, and always drest that Wound; and in about three Months was perfectly cured; but most of the Fleet being sailed before her Recovery, she was left behind, and sent on board the *Tartar Pink*, which then lay in the Harbour, where she remained, doing the Duty of a Sailor, till the Return of the Fleet from *Madrass* when she was turned over to the *Eltham*, Captain *Lloyd* Commander, and sailed for *Bombay*, where they arrived in about ten Days, being scarce of Hands, having only eight in a Watch, of which she was one; and what made their Fatigue still more, was their being obliged to keep continually at the Pump, the Ship having sprung a Leak in her Larboard Bow.

AT *Bombay* they were obliged to heave the Ship down in Order to clean her Bottom, which kept them there about five Weeks, and then they sailed to*Monserrat*, to take the *Royal Duke Indiaman* under Convoy, to bring her to Fort St. *David*'s where she was gone for Provisions.

AT *Bombay* her Master being on Shore, she was obliged to watch in her turn, as is usual on such Occasions; but being one Night on Duty, Mr. *Allen*, who then had the Command of the Ship, being on Shore, desired her to sing for him, which she begged that he would excuse, as she was not very well; but he being proud in this his new Employ, as Commander, absolutely commanded her to sing; which she refused to do, as she did not think it any incumbent Duty for a Soldier to sing when commanded so to do, and that by one who was not an Officer in their Core, or had she any Obligations to him; however this Refusal proved of fatal Consequence to her; he ordered her immediately into Irons, which accordingly was done, and continued for the Space of five Days, and then ordered her to have a dozen Lashes, which she had at the Gang-Way of the Ship, and after that sent to the Foretop-mast-head, for four Hours; such is the Cruelty of those that are invested with Power, and do not know how to use it. However, this Man's Cruelty did not go unpunished; for after there Arival in*England*, as they were unriging the Ship, one of the Sailors let a Block fall on his Head, which hurt him greatly.

THEY now, with the *Royal Duke*, sailed from *Montserrat* to Fort St. *David*'s, and was there at the Time of the great Hurricane, when the *Namur* and*Pembroke*, and other Ships were lost: The *Eltham*, of which she was on board, had some Share in the said Hurricane, for she broke her Cables, and was forced to Sea; but happily returned in again to the Port without receiving any great Damage.

Now during her stay here at Fort St. *David*'s, she had frequent Opportunities, and Causes for Reflection: She went on Shore sundry Times along with some of the Men, where her Ears and her Eyes were often affected with the disagreeable Sound of horrible Oaths, and many lewd Actions and Gestures, such as stripping themselves naked, when they went to swim, a Sight, which however disagreeable it might appear to her, yet she was forced to make a Virtue of Necessity, by openly conforming herself to those rude, indiscreet, and unwomanly Actions, which she silently disfavoured and contemned. But here the unpolished Tars had not Opportunities of extending their Wickedness to such a high Pitch as they would have done, had they had Objects to satiate their brutish Appetites; for there were but a few white Women in the Place; however she saw too much not to be afflicted, lest her Sex should by their impudent, and unlimited Behaviour, be discovered, and her Virtue sacrificed to their rapacious, boundless and lustful Appetites; but Innocency and Virtue is the safest Protection in the worst of Times; and this was what sheltered her from the much dreaded Calamity that threatned her.

ON the 19th of *November* last, the *Eltham* sailed with the rest of the Fleet from Fort St. *David*'s, and kept Company till they came to the Cape of *Good Hope*; when the *Eltham* had Orders to make the best of her Way to *Lisbon*, to take in Money for the Use of the Merchants of *London*.

THE Day after they left Fort St. *David*'s, her Master Lieutenant *Wyegate* died, in whose Death she lost the only Friend she had on board, and where to find such another, she knew not: This brought afresh into her Mind the Remembrance of her faithless Husband, whole Villainy and Cruelty had drove her to all the Straits, Hardships and Dangers she endured both by Sea and Land, and had reduced her to the wretched State she was then in. These Reflections were sufficient to have sunk the Spirits of the most hardy Hero; but she bore them with a becoming Resignation. She was distinguished amongst the Ship's Crew for her Ingenuity in washing and mending of Linnen, but as it is common on board of King's Ships to have some Men who are dexterous at such Performances, she was not suspected upon that Score.

SOME Time after the Death of Lieutenant *Wyegate*, she was taken into the Service of Lieutenant *Kite*, second Lieutenant of the Ship, and continued so about two Months; when he getting a Boy, he recommended her to Mr. *Wallace*, third Lieutenant of the Ship, who proved also a very good Master to her. But now she was laid open (though contrary to her Inclination) to the Company of the Sailors, for they were used, when she had her Head shaved, to enquire why she did not shave her Beard; her Answer was, that she was too young. Upon which they used to damn her, calling her Miss *Molly Gray*, she used to return the uncivil Compliment, by damning them, and telling them, that she could prove herself, as she had always done, during the Voyage, as good a Man as any Seaman on board, and that she would lay them a Wager upon that Point.

DURING this long Voyage, they often used, as I have just said, on account of her smooth Face, to burlesque her, by swearing she was a Woman. This Expression, however indifferently they meant it, gave her abundance of Trouble; she foresaw what the Consequence would be, in case this Joke was carried too far; to prevent which, she with a masculine but modest Assurance, told them, that if they would lay any Wager, she would give them ocular Demonstration of her being as much a Man as the best in the Ship; which Reply had the desired Effect, seeing it put a Stop to their further Suggestions: Next, they began to declare her to be a Woman on account of her smooth Face, seeing she had no Beard; but she told them that she was so very young, that it could not be supposed she should have a Beard so soon; however, she could not prevent their calling her by the Name of *Molly Gray*, which Appellation she went by during the Voyage, until they arrived at *Lisbon*.

WHILE they lay at *Lisbon*, she often went on Shore in Company with the Ships Crew, upon Parties of Pleasure, and was always their Companion in their Revellings; this Part she acted, not out of Choice, but for wise Ends. She remember'd in what Manner she had been reflected upon by them during the Voyage from St. *David*'s to *Lisbon*, therefore she pointed out this Method as the most effectual, to prevent any further suspicious *Reflections for the future*. She very wisely judged, that by associating herself with them, by shewing a free and chearful Disposition, and by being ready to come into their Measures, she should banish from their Imaginations the least Suspicion of her being a Woman, and by that Means enjoy a free and uninterrupted Passage to her native Country, without discovering her Sex. There was one of the Ship's Crew, named *Edward Jefferies*, an intimate Acquaintance, a Marine, and Mess-mate of her's; they two had contracted an Acquaintance and Familiarity with two young Women in *Lisbon*, the handsomest of which was the favourite of our Heroine; but *Jefferies* taking a greater liking to her Choice than his own, proposed to toss up who should have her, which she readily agreed to, not caring how soon she should be rid of such a Companion: This *Jefferies* on tossing up gained the Lady, upon which she readily resigned her into his Hands, and made that serve as a good Excuse for being rid of them both. This Intimacy subsisted between them and the *Portugueze* Women while they remained at *Lisbon*, and when they were about to set sail for *England*, their Sweethearts came to the Ship's side in order to take Leave of them, but was prevented from coming on board, by the Command of the Captain.

WE shall leave the candid Reader at liberty to judge the Disorders, Terrors and Distractions that so many various Scenes must have plunged her into; such a Disquiet, that she had not felt the like in all her past Enterprizes. A thousand Inquietudes rolled in upon her, like so many Billows, and almost sunk her down into the Abyss of Despair. She began to reflect upon the many Vicissitudes she had underwent, since her first launching out into the boisterous Sea of War, occasioned by the Cruelty of a perfidious Husband. What Dangers, what Hardships, and what Fatigues she had underwent! The many Inconveniences she had overcome, and the Difficulties she had surmounted, in preserving her Virtue untainted in the midst of so many vicious and prophane Actions, as had often been represented in their blackest Sable to her view, and that she had hitherto come off Conqueress, and when almost at the Door of her native Country, unsullied and undefiled by any of these Temptations wherewith she had been assaulted; then to be in the greatest Danger; then to have that Virtue, which had hitherto been her assistant and comfortable Companion in all her adverse Fortune, tore from her Breast, and nothing left behind but Shame, Guilt and Confusion. These Reflections had almost vanquished her great Spirit, had not her good Genius led her to put in Practice the Scheme she had formed at *Lisbon*, which answered the End she aimed at, and by which her Virtue, which was always dear to her, remains still untainted, to her immortal Praise.

ON the Affair of the Supply of the Men they had from the *Sheerness* Privateer at *Madeira*, she gave the following Account; which was, that after they were come on board the *Swallow* Sloop, some of them seemed very pensive; so that her Curiosity led her to enquire into the Reason of their Grief, which she found was occasioned by their being brought on board a Man of War, which at first to her seemed strange, not being acquainted with the Manner of Men being impressed; and having often conversed with some of them, found they were sent on board by Force; and some of them having Wives and Children in *England*, and some in *Ireland*, the Thoughts of their long Separation from their Wives and Families, and the uncertainty of ever seeing them again, was the chief Cause of their Sorrows.

THIS Relation, and the Anxieties some of them shewed, gave her new Matter of Contemplation, and often, when retired in her Master's Cabin, reflected on her own Fate, having herself been married to a most faithless Man, who had left her in the utmost Distress, at a Time she was not able to help herself, and that without any Reason, but what was occasioned by his own Extravagances. But here she found the Difference in that Sex, and that greater then she ever conceived before: Here she saw Men in the greatest Affliction, for being forced from them they loved; offering there all for Liberty to return to their native Land and Families, whilst her perfideous Husband's chief Care was to avoid her. However, it was some Consolation to her, in these her distressed Circumstances, to find some on board, and who she concluded must be her Companions as Shipmates, inspired with Sentiments of Honour and Virtue; she also reflected on the unhappy Circumstances of those poor Women and Children these Men had left behind, and often wished she could have an Opportunity of relating to them what she now saw; imagining from her own Case, that it would be some Consolation to them to hear so great Proof of their Affections. She at first blamed them for going to Sea on board the Privateer, but when she was informed that it was only for a little Time, and they not bound to serve longer, than a certain Time specified in their Articles, and that their chief Motives was to serve their Families; in so doing she looked on them as real Objects of Compassion, which occasioned her to sympathize with them; and though Fortune had been so unkind to herself, she could not refrain thinking of theirs, and often endeavoured to asswage their Sorrows, by recommending to them Hopes of a happy Return to *England*; and also procured every Thing which she thought necessary for them on board, which was somewhat in her Power, having Recourse to all her Master's Stores, especially his Liquors, which was pretty plentiful at that Time.

I SHALL depart a little from the Subject, and give the Reader an Account of that basest of Men, our Heroine's Husband, who upon deserting his lawful Wife, entered himself as a Foremast Man on board one of his Countrymen, then lying in the River *Thames*. But where can the guilty Criminal fly for Sanctuary? His own Conscience must prove his Executioner, and a thousand Monitors within, who Vulture like, always gnaw the Liver, not suffering the Mind to enjoy the shortest Interval of Quiet; this admirable Truth has been fully verified in him, according to the most substantial Circumstances, as shall hereafter be made appear.

ONE Day at *Lisbon*, on her Return to *England*, falling in Company with many of her Ship-mates, they all went into an *Irish* House, by the *Romanado*'s, to drink some Wine, where was sitting at the same Time an *Englishman*, a Sailor, who had lately come from *Genoa* on board a *Dutch* Vessel; there were some of his Brother Tars in Company who knew him; upon which they became very merry, and began, over their Glass and their Pipe, to talk over some of their Adventures, and what they met with in their Travels worthy taking Notice of; and she, acoording to her constant Practice, was enquiring amongst the Mariners if any of them knew one *James Summs*, who, she said, had formerly been an intimate Acquaintance of her's; upon which this Stranger broke Speech, and told 'em of an Affair that happened at *Genoa* while he was there. There was, says he, a *Dutchman* of that Name, a Sailor, imprisoned there, for stabbing a Native of the Place, a Person of some Distinction, with a Knife, of which Wound he soon expired; I, with two or three more of our Countrymen appointed to go and visit him under this his Misfortune, which we accordingly did: When we came to the Place, we were introduced by a Kind of Officer, where he lay in a melancholy Situation; but upon our entering the Room, he raised himself up from the Place where he had reclined his Head, and saluted us in *English*; then we began to condole his Misfortune: Upon which, finding us affected with his melancholy Situation, and the cruel Punishment he was about to suffer, he spoke to us in the following Manner. Gentlemen, The Crime I am to die for I committed, therefore my Punishment will be just whenever it falls: But this is not the only Crime I stand indicted for at the Bar of that All-seeing Judge, who searches into the innermost Recesses of our most concealed Actions, and who pursues the Guilty where-ever they go; I, who am here condemned for Murder, a few Years ago lived in *Wapping, London*, my Name is *James Summs*, a *Dutchman* by Birth; I married a young Woman there, named *Hannah Snell*, born in *Worcester*, but who then lodged with a Brother-in-Law, a Carpenter in *Ship-street*: We had not been long joined in Matrimony before she proved with Child; and I, forgetting my Duty as a Husband, and an approaching Father, gave a loose to my vicious Inclinations, eloped from the Partner of my Bed, and the one half of myself, went and took up my Residence amongst a Parcel of lewd, base Women, who withdrew my Affections entirely from her, who had the only just Title to it; and to satisfy their insatiable and extravagant Demands, I drained her of her all. This proved only the Downfall to my future Calamities; for my Substance being now exhausted, thrust out of Doors by these *Ladies of Pleasure*, who proved to me *Ladies of Pain*, and being ashamed to look my much injured Wife in the Face any more, whom I had so basely betrayed, my Mind was rack'd with exquisite Torture, so that I would willingly have fled from myself if it had been possible. A thousand Inventions came into my Head how I should dispose of myself at this critical Juncture. I employed all the Skill I was master of to be assisting in extricating me out of this Dilemma; at last I resolved to go on board one Ship or other, in order to make a Voyage.

THE first Ship I boarded was a *Rotterdam* Trader, who accepted me in the Capacity of a Sailor, having but few Hands, the Steersman agreed to give me 40 Guilders *per* Month. A few Days afterwards we made down with the Tide, and sailed over to *Rotterdam*, where we unloaded: We had not been many Days here, before an unforeseen Accident happened, which was like to have produced fatal Consequences: One of the Boys going one Day into the Steerage with a lighted Candle, where was some Powder loose; a Spark from the Candle dropt into the

Powder, which in an Instant blew up, and did great Damage to the Vessel. This Accident was charged upon me by two of the Men who bore me a Grudge; upon which I was Keel-haul'd, and received many Lashes besides. This ill Usage provoked me much, so that I determined to quit my Master's Service, and let him know that I intended to leave him; upon which he paid me my Wages, and we parted. I then entered myself on board an *Irish* Merchant, bound to *Lisbon*, which Voyage I performed, and returned to *Cork*, the Place where the Cargo was to be disposed of.

HERE, after I had received my Wages, I was discharged, and falling into bad Company, my Wages was soon spent, and being without Money, Cloaths or Friends, in a strange Country, made my Case very deplorable, which brought into my Mind, my wicked Proceedings to my dear Wife, and I lookt upon those Afflictions I underwent, as a just Punishment from Heaven, for my wicked Actions; however, these Reflections soon gave Way to Self-preservation; I was in great Distress, and how to work my Deliverance, was the main Subject of my Thoughts; at the very same Time, there was a *Portuguese* Vessel lying in the Harbour, bound to *Genoa*; they wanted a few Hands, some of their own Men having died in the Voyage; I proffered my Service; they accepted of me, staid in*Cork*, a few Days afterwards, then weighed Anchor, and set sail for *Genoa*, where we arrived in Safety in about three Weeks; here we had not continued long, before I perpetrated the Murther, for which I am about to suffer: Now Gentlemen, I have given you a full Account of the most material Incidents that has happened to me since I left *England*, I therefore earnestly intreat the Favour of you, when once you return to *England*, to enquire after my Wife, and if you find her, be pleased in my Name, to present her the Love of a dying Husband, who conscious of his Guilt, humbly begs her Pardon and Forgiveness, for all the Injuries he hath done her, since first he knew her; this his Request we promised to fulfill, if once we returned to *England*; so we took our last Farewel. None of us, ever saw him afterwards, but were informed, that he was sewed up in a Sack, with heavy Stones, and thrown into the Sea; the other two *Englishmen*sailed for *Leghorn*, and I for this Place, and when I go Home, I intend to make an Enquiry concerning the said Woman: She listened attentively all the While he was relating this Story, and weighing all the particular Circumstances of this Relation, she perceived so many concurring Circumstances blended together, as put it beyond all Doubt he was her Husband; this Account however, notwithstanding his vile Proceedings, grieved her much, and no doubt would have broke forth into briny Tears, had she been in a Place of Retirement: She sometimes grieved at his cruel and untimely Fate, but suddenly, the ill Treatment she met with from him, returned triumphant in her Mind, and extinguished her kindled Tenderness: However, she told the Sailor who related this

Story, that from the Account he gave of this Man, he must have been the same identical Person, with whom she had formerly been acquainted, and if once she came to *England*, she would endeavour to find out the Wife of this unfortunate Man, whom she knew very well, and would acquaint her with this Catastrophe, and by so saying, concealed herself entirely from the least Suspicion.

H A V I N G now finished the Account of her Husbands untimely End, as related to her at *Lisbon*; the Detail of which, appeared to her, as if sent from above, to free her from those anxious Cares, which, in the midst of the greatest Dangers, always set triumphant in her Breast, I shall now proceed to her Voyage from thence to *England*.

T H E Y set sail from *Lisbon* the 3d of *May*, and arrived at *Spithead* the 1st of *June*, without any Thing material during the Voyage (which was lengthened by Calms and contrary Winds); that very Day she arrived at *Spithead* she came on Shore, and took a Lodging along with several of her Shipmates and Marines, at one *James Cunningham*'s, at the Sign of the *Jolly Marine* and *Sailor*; where the House being thronged with Lodgers, she was obliged to be Bedfellow to one *John Huchins*, a Brother Marine, the first Night; but during her short Stay in *Portsmouth*, in her often Rovings in and about the Town, (which was only two Days and three Nights) she happen'd to meet with the Sister of Mr. *Cunningham*, the Drum-Major's Wife, one *Catherine* ——, with whom she had cultivated a slender Acquaintance at the Time she first enlisted there. This young Woman knew *Hannah* to be the young Soldier that had enlisted and been sent abroad with Admiral *Boscawen*, and expressed some Joy at her safe Return: Then entering into this Conversation, introduced a farther Intimacy; and *Hannah*, rather than sit to drink with her Shipmates, spent most of her Time with this young Woman. This Opportunity improved their Conversation, and sometimes they conversed upon Love; and *Hannah* finding this young Woman had no dislike to her, she endeavoured to try if she could not act the Lover as well as the Soldier, which she so well effected, that it was agreed upon she should return from *London*, in order to be married as soon as she had got her Discharge and Pay; and tho' but so short a Time there as two Days, had effected this her Amour so as to obtain the young Woman's Consent to marry her.

In order to countenance this her Scheme, she told the supposed Object of her Love, that as soon as she arrived at *London*, and received her Wages, she would remit the same to her; and when she had visited, and tarried some time with each of her nigh Relations and intimate Friends, she would then return to *Portsmouth*, according to Agreement, and consummate their matrimonial Ceremonies with a Solemnity suitable to her Abilities.

THE next Night, being *Saturday* the 2d of *June*, *Hannah*'s Bedfellow, who had lain with her the Night before, went out of Town, and one *James Moody*, who had been a Ship-mate with her on board the *Eltham* from Fort St. *David*'s to *England*, coming in the Evening of that Day, and wanting a Lodging, he was received by the Landlord, and as *Hannah* was his intimate, he was admitted to be her Bedfellow, which continued for two Nights together, without the least Suspicion in Life.

IT is here worthy of Observation, that this Woman should lay three Nights with two different Men, one of whom who had been her Companion and Fellow-adventurer, during the Space of fifteen Months and more; and never, during that Space of Time, discover the least Hint of her being of the female Kind; and this Man had often been her Assistant in the most dangerous Exploits, and could not avoid acknowledging, that she behaved upon all Occasions, with the greatest Bravery and Resolution.

WHITMONDAY, being the 4th of *June*, she set out from *Portsmouth* for *London*; accompanied by *George Orley*, a Serjeant of Marines, who was a Partner with her in her Adventures, and who, together with nine Marines, accompanied her to *London*: She received before they set out from *Portsmouth*, five Shillings Conduct-money. The first Place she traveled to after her departure from *Portsmouth*, was *Petersfield*, in *Hampshire*; where she lay all Night, with one *Andrew Gray* a Marine, not only in the same Regiment, but in the same Company: Next Day travel'd as far as *Guildford*, where the aforesaid *Andrew Gray* and she were Bedfellows; next Night she arrived in *London*, where she disingaged herself from her old Intimates, and lodged along with her Brother, Mr. *James Gray*, Carpenter, in *Ship-Street, Wapping*; where she now resides.

Now I have brought my female Adventurer home again to her native Country, after near five Years Adventures; prompted thereto by the ill Usage of a faithless Husband, who, after first stripping her of her all, and then eloping, prompted her to the Resolution of disguising herself, by putting on Men's Apparel, going into the Country without the Knowledge of her Brother, Sister, or any other of her Friends, in search of him who had thus abused her; and entering into Colonel *Guise*'s Regiment of Foot, then lying at *Coventry*, who from thence marched to *Carlisle*, where she was ill used, the Particulars of which, are set forth at large in the foregoing Pages: How she received five hundred Lashes at *Carlisle*, as a Punishment for her virtuous Conduct, her Resolution to desert, and her puting this Determination into Execution; her changing her military Cloathing about a Mile from Town, for the rustick Garb of a Shepherd; her Arrival at *Portsmouth*, her entering into General *Fraser*'s Regiment of Marines, her being draughted out for the *East Indies*; her embarking on board the *Swallow* Sloop of War, under the

Command of Admiral *Boscawen*, and the many Vicissitudes she underwent during the Series of her Adventures, until her safe (though unexpected) return to her Native Country, where, after her Arrival, she met with sundry humorous Incidents; with many other material Circumstances, the Particulars of which is here set down at large; but not to swell this Treatise with any Thing fictitious or doubtful, I have asserted nothing but plain Matter of Fact as here set down.

I would have my candid Readers survey in Imagination, the many various Scenes that here display themselves with a most surprizing Lustre. Here is a Woman, and an *English* Woman, who, notwithstanding the many Dangers and Vicissitudes she underwent for near the Space of five Years, during her Travels, was never found out to be of the feminine Gender. It is true many threatned Discoveries were attempted by her Shipmates and Fellow-Adventurers, which derived its Influence from her not having a Beard; but her ready Turns of Mind undeceived all those who shewed themselves overbusy in prying into this Secret: This her Conduct, very surprizingly preserved her Virtue from becoming a Sacrifice to the Impetuosity of the carnal Desires of both her Superiors and Inferiors; for can it be imagined, that in the midst of so many Dangers, where there was no Back-Door to creep out at, if her Sex had been discovered, but she must have fallen a Victim to the loose, disorderly, and vitious Appetites of many on board, especially those whom she was more immediately concerned with, to wit, her Officers. These Reflections must possess the Reader with generous Sentiments of this our Heroine, who by her Subtilty, and ready Inventions, destroyed in the Embrio, every Thing advanced by her Fellow-Shipmates, that she imagined might be a Means of exposing her Virtue.

S U C H an Adventure as this, is not to be met with in the Records of either antient or modern Observations, therefore, for the Sake of the *British* Nation, ought to be recorded in Golden Characters on a Statue of Marble for succeeding Ages, to peruse with Admiration, that an *English* Woman should, *Amazon* like, not only enter herself upon the List in behalf of her Country at Home, but boldly and resolutely launch out into the most remote Corners of the Earth, upon enterprizing and dangerous Adventures, the like never attempted before by any of her Sex, even daring Fate, as it were, to execute her most rigorous Inflictions upon her; the many Struglings and Conflicts she encounter'd during the Course of her Travels, not being used to the watery Element, and the many Revolutions that often happen upon the Surface of the Deep; the many Duties she was obliged to execute, in the midst of Hundreds of the most unpolite Part of Mankind, such as Tars; the many Fears and Suspicions she harboured least her Sex should be discovered, to avoid which, she proved her own Physician, in extracting the Ball out of her Wound, to prevent that Discovery which must unavoidably have happened, had she permitted the Surgeons to have performed their regular Operations: These, with many more, (seemingly insurmountable Difficulties) did this our *British* Heroine undergo, and overcome, by her safe Arrival in her native Country, as before-mentioned.

WHEN she arrived in *London*, she went to her Brother in Law's House, in *Ship-Street, Wapping*; where he lived at the Time when she went abroad; she no sooner entered the House, than her Sister (notwithstanding her Disguise) knew her, but her Brother in Law, Mr. *Gray* being in Bed, she went to his Bedside, being desirous to see him, where he lay in a Slumber, and embraced him, upon which he awoke, and seeing a Person in a Soldier's Dress, coming to his Bedside in such a Manner and imbracing him, surprised him much, however, he was soon freed from this Surprize by her discovering herself, which afforded him a great deal of Satisfaction; as she was his great Favourite before she went abroad, and her sudden and unexpected Appearance, caused a great deal of Joy, in the whole Family; after refreshing herself with a Part of what the House afforded, she diverted her Brother and Sister 'till Bed-time, with some Part of her Adventures, which relation forced Tears from their Eyes.

THERE was at this Time a Female Lodger in Mr. *Gray*'s House, of whom Mr. *Gray* requested, that she would admit a Sister of his for a Bedfellow, to which she readily agreed: But when the Sister was introduced, the young Woman, who was then in Bed, was very much surprized to see a Soldier sit down to undress himself in her Bed-Chamber; but Mr. *Gray* and his Wife discovered the Secret, which, notwithstanding, she would not Credit, until she had occular Demonstration. This was the first, next to her Brother and Sister, that she discovered herself to, and ever since they have been Bedfellows, which made the Neighbours report (imagining her to be a Man) that the young Woman was married to a Soldier, and this great Untruth was reported for Fact throughout the whole Neighbourhood.

SOMETIME after this, she, in Company with her Sister and supposed Wife, went to *Westminster*, in order to see her Friends, who were very much dissatisfy'd at her carrying a strange Woman in Company with her supposed Brother, who perhaps, upon receiving his Money, might decoy him into some Place of bad Fame, where he might chance to lose it all in an Instant. This, together with some former Passages, constrains me to observe how much the Publick, both at Home and Abroad, have been deceived in this Woman, she being so long in the Army and Navy, where there were many penetrating clear-sighted Gentlemen, and ashore in foreign Countries amongst Men, Women and Children; and notwithstanding all these publick Characters, her Sex not discovered. This must cause Admiration in every Reader; but she counterfeited the Man so dextrously, and does to this very

Day, that the most excellent Judge of Features, Semetry or Gesture, cannot discover the Deceit.

B U T that I may not suffer any of my inquisitive Readers to remain in suspence concerning some particular Adventures that befel her, the bare Relation of which may not be altogether so satisfactory, I shall explain those which appear most Paradoxical, in order not only to satisfy every Reader, but also to prevent any future Reflexions that might occasionally arise from such a Neglect.

W H E N she first enter'd into the Service at *Coventry*, she marched to *Carlisle*, where she was Whipt for Neglect of Duty, being unjustly accused by Serjeant*Davis*, as is fully mentioned in the preceding Pages. The Method she used to prevent the Discovery of her Sex was this, according to her own Declaration: Her Breasts were then not so big by much as they are at present, her Arms being extended and fixed to the City Gates, her Breasts were drawn up, and consequently did not appear so large; and besides this, her Breast was to the Wall, and could not be discovered by any of her Comrades; and when she was Whipt on board, her Hands being lashed to the Gangway, she stood upright, and tied a Handkerchief round her Neck, to prevent, as it were, any Lashes that she might accidentally receive there, to conceal her Breasts, which were covered by the Ends of the Handkerchief falling over them, and thereby prevented a Discovery which must unavoidably have happened, had not she thus acted. And what the Consequences of such an unravell'd Secret would have produced, she was at a Loss to imagine, the Thoughts of which perplexed her incessantly; however, she escaped being discovered at this Juncture also, as well as at many more, when she imagined herself in the most imminent Dangers: But all those adverse Turns gave an Edge to her Inventions, and by that means extricated her out of the many Difficulties she was involved in.

T H I S the Reader may plainly perceive throughout the whole Narration; and I am convinced, that no Age or Country, ever produced a more distinguished Instance of Virtue, Conduct and Resolution, than is to be met with in this our Heroine's Adventures, which is worthy to be transmitted to latest Posterity; to inform succeeding Ages, that such an Instance of Heroism was not to be found in the *British* Annals, that the like could not be met with, in the Observations of any Nation in the World, that a Woman, whose mould is tender, delicate and unable to endure Fatigues, and who is terrified at the Name of Dangers, should undergo so many Scenes without relinquishing her Resolution of keeping her Sex a Secret.

I H A D forgot to mention a Circumstance worthy of Notice, in its proper Place, which happened at *Lisbon*, concerning the two Sweethearts, she and *Edward Jefferies* had there, as is before mentioned; which was, that when she and *Jefferies* were on board before they set sail from *Lisbon* to *England*, these two young Women, of whom mention is made, came along the Ship's Side in a Boat, and called for *James Grey*, and she being informed thereof, went into the Boat where they were, but after a little Conversation, she found them inclined to come on board, and remain there while they lay in the River; she promised to ask Leave of the Captain for their Reception, but a fresh and seasonable Thought came into her Head, which was, that if they came on board, and continued any Time, they might sooner discover her than any of the Men, therefore to prevent the worst, instead of pleading for their Admittance, she requested of the Captain, that they should not be suffered to come on board. This Request was not only intended for her own Preservation, but likewise to preserve the Women from being debauched by the Sailors, which they could not have avoided, had they came on board; by which Means, both she and they escaped the threatned Danger.

I KNOW the Reader will be desirous to know how the Ball was extracted out of her Groin, and will imagine, that it was next to an Impossibility it could be performed without a Discovery. Now to rectify the Scruples of such, I shall relate this Account as attested by herself; which she said was, that after she received the twelve Wounds, as before mentioned, she remained all that Day, and the following Night in the Camp, before she was carried to the Hospital, and after she was brought there, and laid in a Kit, she continued till next Day in the greatest Agony and Pain, the Ball still remaining in the Flesh of that Wound in her Groin, and how to extract it she knew not, for she had not discovered to the Surgeons that she had any other Wound than those in her Legs. This Wound being so extreme painful, it almost drove her to the Precipice of Despair; she often thought of discovering herself, that by that Means she might be freed from the unspeakable Pain she endured, by having the Ball taken out by one of the Surgeons; but that Resolution was soon banished, and she resolved to run all Risques, even at the hazard of her Life, rather than that her Sex should be known. Confirmed in this Resolution, she communicated her Design to a black Woman, who attended upon her, and could get at the Surgeons Medicines, and desired her Assistance; and her Pain being so very great, that she was unable to endure it much longer, she intended to try an Experiment upon herself, which was, to endeavour to extract the Ball out of that Wound; but notwithstanding she discovered her Pain and Resolution to this Black, yet she did not let her know that she was a Woman. The Black readily came, and afforded her all the Assistance she could, by bringing her Lint and Salve to dress the Wound with, which she had recourse to, it being left in the Wards where the Patients lay; for which Act of Friendship she made her a Present of a Rupee at her Departure, which is 3*s.* 4*d.* of the Currency of that Country, but here in *England* it goes for no more than 2*s.* 6*d.* Now the Manner in which she extracted the Ball was full hardy and desperate: She prob'd the Wound with her Finger till she came where the Ball lay, and then upon feeling it, thrust in both her Finger and Thumb, and pulled it out. This was a very rough Way of proceeding with ones own Flesh; but of two Evils, as she thought, this was the least, so rather chusing to have her Flesh tore and mangled than her Sex discovered. After this Operation was performed, she applied some of the healing Salves which the Black had brought her, by the help of which she made a perfect Cure of that dangerous Wound.

THE Reader will here observe, the invincible Courage and Resolution of this Woman, who in the midst of so many Inconveniences as she daily encounter'd, should still be able to guard herself from a discovery of her Sex; but indeed it appears she acted so artfully on every Emergency, as rendered any Attempts of this Kind abortive; for notwithstanding the Wound she received in her Groin was the most dangerous of all the others, yet that was the only Wound she kept from the Knowledge of the Surgeons, by telling them, when they came to examine her, that all the Wounds she had received were in her Legs which they readily believed; and by that Means prevented any farther Search.

OBSERVE here the Steadiness and Intrepidity wherewith she overcame all the Pains and Dangers which assaulted her. Who would not in the midst of so much Agony and Pain as she felt here, broke through the strongest and most virtuous Resolutions in order to obtain immediate Relief? But she remained still inflexible in the midst of every Affliction wherewith she was environed, no Consideration could ever prevail upon her in her own Mind to deviate from the Resolutions she had imbibed upon her first Launching out, and which, though it cost her many a painful Hour, yet by her steady Adherence to these Principles, she obtained a Conquest over near five Years adverse Fortune.

NOW having satisfied the Reader's Doubts in Regard to the Methods she used to conceal her Sex from the Knowledge of any about her, on these particular Occasions, when she was most exposed, *viz.* the twice she was whipt, and upon the dressing of her Wounds, which were Times I say, when Danger was at the Door ready to burst in, and plunder the Habitation of its most valuable Furniture; I shall next proceed, to shew the Reader some Transactions that has occur'd since she came to *London*.

THO' she had not discovered her Sex to any besides her Brother in Law, her Sister, and the young Woman with whom she lodged; she was very uneasy, fearing, lest a further Discovery should be made, and she thereby deprived of her Soldier's Pay. This Motive induced her to conceal herself as much as possible, till she had received her Pay, (being 15 Pounds) which she accordingly did on the *Saturday* after her Arrival in *London*, being the 9th Day of *June*, when she, with Serjeant *Orley, John Hutchins, James Moody, Andrew Grey*, and the rest of the Marines that came to *London* with her, went to the Agent *John Winter*, Esq; in *Downing-Street, Westminster*; where being all paid and discharged, they went to an Alehouse, the Fighting-Cocks, next Door to Mr. *Winter*'s House, and there she first discovered herself to her Comrades. There being two Suits of Cloathing due to her from the Regiment, she also sold them for 16*s.* being glad to get hold of all the Money she could before her Sex was discovered.

Now upon receiving her Pay, and all her fellow Adventures then present, she thought that was the most proper Opportunity she ever could have, for disclosing her Sex, seeing they could then testify the Truth of all the Fatigues, Dangers and other Incidents of her Adventures, and that her Sex was never discovered, which if then omitted, she might never have an Opportunity of seeing them all together again, and by that Means, the Account of her Adventures as aforesaid, might be lookt upon by the Publick as fictitious: These Considerations prevailed upon her to embrace the then seasonable Occasion, for discovering herself, before they took a final Leave; she therefore proposed to them to make merry before they parted, which was agreed to by one and all of them, as they expected never to meet altogether any more; and then she discovered herself to the whole Company which caused a universal Surprise amongst them all.

BUT after they had recovered themselves from this sudden Emotion, which the aforesaid surprizing Information had thrown them into, they could hardly be prevailed upon to believe the Truth of what she advanced, until her Brother and Sister undeceived them, by informing them of the whole Transaction. Upon which, they all with one Voice sounded forth her Praise, by applauding her Courage as a Soldier, her Dexterity as a Sailor, her humane Deportment and Sincerity as a Friend, having performed many good Offices towards them in Times of their Sickness, and upon every other Opportunity. They expatiated much upon the Evenness of her Temper, the Regularity of her Conduct, and the many Dangers and Hardships she underwent, without ever shewing the least sign of Discontent with her Situation. These Encomiums once over, the forementioned *Moody*, who had been her Bedfellow two Nights, and was present at this Discovery, became of a sudden so much enamoured with her, that he proposed to marry her, which she refused, upon reflecting what a bad Husband she formerly had, and who had been the Instrument of all her Misfortunes, therefore for his sake she resolved, in the Mind she was then in, never to engage with any Man living.

NOW upon the Discovery of her Sex, her Relations, and some of her intimate Friends, advised her to apply by a Petition to his Royal Highness the Duke of *Cumberland*, not doubting but that his Highness would make some proper

Provision for her, as she had received so many Wounds. Upon which a Petition was drawn up, setting forth her Adventures, and the Hardships she underwent, together with the many Wounds she received, which she was the Bearer of herself, and coming where his Royal Highness then was in his Landau, accompanied by Colonel *Napier*, she delivered her Petition to his Royal Highness, and upon his perusing it, gave it to the Colonel, desiring him to enquire into the Merits. So that it is not doubted but his Royal Highness will make her some handsome Allowance, exclusive of *Chelsea* College, to which she is entitled.

N O W , notwithstanding this our Heroine has at sundry Times appeared upon a publick Stage since her Return to *England*, and diverted the Auditors with a Song or two, in order to procure a little Money, wherewith to support her present necessary Expences, yet the Publick we hope will encourage her, if she should have a Benefit Play perform'd on her own Account, as an Encouragement for the many singular Adventures, and signal Deliverances from the many Perils and Dangers that environed her, and all in the Behalf of her Country: Her Merit I think is such as is sufficient to set her upon a Level with the most celebrated Ladies of antient Times. She is not to be put in the Lists with the fictitious and fabulous Stories of a *Pamella*, &c. no, her Virtues have displayed their Lustre in the remotest Corner of the World, the once fam'd *Asia*. It was here she performed such noble Deeds, as will cause her Name and Fame to be revered to latest Posterity: Here is the real *Pamella* to be to found, who in the midst of thousands of the Martial Gentry, preserved her Chastity by the most virtuous Stratagems that could be devised: Next behold her upon the Ocean, surrounded with Storms, Tempests and Hurricanes, every Moment expecting the watery Element should prove her Tomb; and as an Addition to her wretched Situation, she was intermixed with the hardy resolute Tars, who soon would have batter'd down the Fort of her Virtue, had they discovered that *James Gray* was Mrs. *Hannah Snell*. See her making for fair *Asia*'s ancient Shore, with all the speed that Canvas Wings could carry her; and going aloft and discharging the Duty of a skilful Mariner; afterwards upon the Poop and Quarter Deck exercising her small Arms, as an able and experienced Soldier: Then when the Enemy were attacked, firing her Pontoons, brandishing her Sword, receiving dangerous Wounds, and spilling her precious Blood: If these, together with many more Circumstances, are not Virtues infinitely surpassing the Adventures and Virtues of our romantick *Pamella*, I own I am mistaken, and shall leave them to the Judgment of the impartial Reader. This is a real *Pamella*; the other a counterfeit; this*Pamella* is real Flesh and Blood, the other is no more than a Shadow: Thefore let this our Heroine, who is the Subject of this History, be both admired and encouraged.

I SHALL conclude this Subject, with observing, that notwithstanding the many Reflections thrown upon the Fair Sex on Account of their Weakness in Point of Secret, the Conduct of our Heroine in this Particular is a plain and demonstrative Proof of this Truth, that a Woman is not only capable of confining a Secret in her Bosom, but actually do so upon sundry Emergences, seeing she concealed her Sex in the midst of the greatest Dangers and Hardships; no Difficulties, no Pains, no Terrors, nor Prospect of future Calamities, could prevail upon her to discover a Secret, which, if once divulged, might have proved more fatal to her Repose, than all the Difficulties she had undergone during the past Course of her Adventures.

THE Adventures of this Female Soldier, as the like is not to be paralleled in History, should never be forgot by our *British* Ladies, but whenever satirized by any of the Masculine Gentry, they should always have this Repartee ready, *Remember* HANNAH SNELL.

I SHALL now conclude with informing the Public, that she still continues to wear her Regimentals; but how she intends to dispose of herself, or when, if ever, to change her Dress, is more than what she at present seems certain of.

AS this Treatise was done in a Hurry from *Hannah Snell*'s own Mouth, and directly committed to the Press, occasioned by the Impatience of the Town to have it published, it is not doubted but that such Part of it as appears somewhat incorrect, will be candidly overlooked, that, being made up in the Veracity and Fullness of her surprising Adventures; the like not to be met with in the Records of Time.

Printed in Great Britain
by Amazon